THE LEADERSHIP LEGACY

THE LEADERSHIP LEGACY

LaQuanda Carpenter, Ed.D.

Mahogany Book Publishing
North Augusta, South Carolina

THE LEADERSHIP LEGACY

Published by
Mahogany Book Publishing

North Augusta, South Carolina
mahoganyintel@gmail.com

LaQuanda Carpenter, Publisher / Editorial Director
Yvonne Rose/QualityPress.info, Book Packager

ALL RIGHTS RESERVED

No part of this book may be reproduced or transmitted in any form or by any means electronic or mechanical, including photocopying, recording, or by any information storage and retrieval system without written permission from the authors, except for the inclusion of brief quotations in a review.

The publication is sold with the understanding that the publisher is not engaged in rendering legal or other professional services. If legal advice or other expert assistance is required, the services of a competent professional person should be sought.

Copyright © 2024 by LaQuanda Carpenter
Paperback ISBN: 979-8-9902060-0-7
Ebook ISBN: 979-8-9902060-1-4
Library of Congress Control Number: 2024904749

DEDICATION

This book is dedicated to the countless individuals and collective units that have poured into me by way of mentorship, leadership, conversation, prayer, and guidance. I am forever grateful to you for the belief that you instilled in me and prayed that I would one day believe it myself.

To the countless educators all over the world who pour their hearts and souls into children every single day, I pray that your hearts and souls are blessed forever.

This guide is for you.

May we continue to forever enrich schools all over the world.

One scholar and one teacher at a time.

ACKNOWLEDGEMENTS

My journey in leadership began with a few amazing people who saw something in me when I did not even know who I was, what I stood for, and what my abilities were, and I am so thankful for these amazing gems.

I am forever grateful for Dr. Amy Carver Burk's love and foresight. She blessed kids every day with her belief in their success.

Dr. Vivian Tolbert Roper's vision for children is remarkable and sincere. She is an amazing school leader who poured into her teachers and students every single day.

My goal of penning a manuscript was shared many times with some dear friends and award-winning authors, such as Keith L. Brown and Stephanie Perry Moore. Neither of them ever lost patience with me. They both always said the same thing, "sit down and write." I thank you both for your encouragement and patience.

I must acknowledge the first book I wrote was with my dear friend Dr. Tova Jackson Davis as we were high school students at the time. It is our goal to dust off our first manuscript and get it in your hands. I acknowledge Tova as she was my first writing partner.

I want to acknowledge any teacher, school employee, and child that I have interacted with in the K-12 space. My prayer is that I was a source of light for you during our time together and I hope that I had a positive impact on your life.

My family has always been a source of encouragement and strength and I am forever grateful for your continuous love.

My children root for me every day and are always happy when good things happen. To my son Landen and my daughter Layla, I hope you are always proud of the fact that I am your mom. It is always my goal to lead, guide, and teach you, even though most times you are teaching me.

CONTENTS

Dedication v
Acknowledgements vii
Contents ix
Preface xi

Part One: Amazing Conversations 1
1. Dr. Amy Carver Burk 3
2. Dr. Vivian Tolbert Roper 9

Part Two: Building Blocks 15
3. My CAREER Start as a Teacher 17
4. My BACKGROUND 20
5. My CALLING 25

Part Three: Strategies 27
6. Stay True to SELF 29
7. Don't Worry About the DATA, Worry About the PEOPLE 32
8. Make School a "SAFE" Space for Everyone 34
9. Be a "BLESSING" to Everyone on This Journey ... 40
10. Walk in With GRATITUDE 46
11. Create a FAMILY 48

12. Be COURAGEOUS 51
13. Take Time to "PAUSE" and "THINK" 53
14. Make it "HEARTWORK"...55
15. Get HELP 58

PREFACE

The purpose of this book is to give school leaders a quick set of strategies and tools that can be embraced and implemented immediately. Having tools in our toolbox that can help schools move from good to great or mediocre to phenomenal should be a goal for all of us. I hope that you have found your purpose by way of teaching, leading, coaching, inspiring, and motivating young people and school staff to be the absolute best version of themselves every single day.

In Service,
LaQuanda Brown Carpenter, Ed.D.

PART ONE
AMAZING CONVERSATIONS

I begin this journey of the *"Leadership Legacy"* by taking a few moments to spend with some key people who influenced me in a way that I am forever thankful to them for our time spent together. My appreciation of these amazing people extends to infinity, for they answered my call and took time out of their busy lives to sit and chat with me. I hope you enjoy and follow these amazing conversations as I share with you "my journey," and "my legacy."

1.

DR. AMY CARVER BURK

In preparation for this book, I was able to spend some time with one of my most favorite teachers of all time, Dr. Burk. She was one of my high school teachers and I am forever grateful for her love and foresight.

Dr. Burk served the Southwest Dekalb High School (Decatur, Georgia) community as an award-winning English teacher. As a high school student, I had the privilege of learning from her for several courses. She had a life-long impact on my life, and I treasure the fact that I was one of her students.

I was able to spend a few moments with Dr. Burk via Zoom. I hope you enjoy our conversation and can learn from it.

LC: *Like so many of my classmates and friends, I am so fortunate to have attended Southwest Dekalb High School (SWD). Historically, this part of Decatur, GA where SWD sits has been one of the most highly economical and influential communities for African-Americans in the United States. Schools in the most eastern part of the city have always operated as examples of Historically Black Colleges and Universities (HBCUs). As a white female teaching in a predominantly African-American high school with such strong black, cultural practices, how did you build relationships and connect with your students?*

ACB: "Over the years, I have thought about this a lot because I can keep up with students on Facebook. Coach Godfrey always told me that we are one race, the human race. I grew up in schools where Black students attended, and several were my friends. I was familiar with Black people, but not Black culture. Southwest Dekalb taught me about culture. I looked students in their eyes, I learned their names. I made connections."

LC: *You taught quite a few different subjects and classes in the English department, and I had the pleasure of sitting in your classroom for several classes. I remember your classroom feeling like "family" and my classmates and I always felt at "home" when we were under your care. There were several semesters when I had your class for fourth period, which was the long block for lunch. Most teachers would tell us to eat school lunch or bring a cold lunch from home. I distinctly remember you allowing us to bring hot food and heat it in the microwave. You gave us access to a microwave, and we all felt super special. I remember loving you for this because many of* us were at school for twelve hours due to our involvement in after-school activities. How did you develop that type of atmosphere and how do you believe that transferred to shaping us to perform at our best?

ACB: "I wanted us to be a team in the yearbook class. I also wanted to give you all the perks that I did not give to other classes. I wanted you all to feel very special because you were on the yearbook staff. I chose you all because I saw something in you that I did not think you had yet recognized in yourselves. I wanted you all to learn your strengths, whether it was organization, photography, writing, creativity, project management, or whatever your specific talent was that would carry over into college or the workforce."

LC: *You asked me to complete the application to serve as a Teacher Cadet at one of the feeder elementary schools. I applied without knowing that I would seriously pursue a career as an educator. How did you identify students for this program? Did you focus on those you believed would pursue the profession?*

ACB: "Some students I knew would be teachers and some students voiced that they wanted to be a teacher. I also wanted to focus on students who I thought may work in child psychology, nursing, the legal field, medicine, and any career that may interact with children. I looked at students who would take it seriously and who were dedicated and responsible. I think the program gave students the chance to explore opportunities to work with children. My goal was to help you all discover your interests as they relate to children and adolescents."

"The program was so exciting, and I was so honored that I was chosen to teach the Teacher Cadet class."

LC: *I remember you getting married and inviting students to your wedding. We were so happy that you had found the love of your life. One of the benefits of social media is that we can stay connected to those that we love and care about, regardless of where we live and how we spend our lives.* What advice would you give to young people who are living during this time of social media?

ACB: "First, I would tell my students not to believe everything they see on social media. You have to still do your own research."

"I would tell my students to be very careful. Be careful about what you put out about yourself. Watch your settings. Block people that are "phishing" for information. Be very cautious."

"When I see my students today on social media and if they use bad grammar, I will still correct them. *That always gets a laugh from students.*"

"The pandemic taught us how to use the internet in a positive way for instructional practices. One assignment that I did when I was still teaching was modeling a Facebook page. If we were reading a novel, I would make a mock Facebook page using one of the characters from the text. The students each would have a role or a character and would have to make comments under posts based on the characterization of the role. I would advise teachers to learn to use social media and teach students how to use it by incorporating current content."

LC: *I want to express my sincere gratitude to you because I know that you positively influenced me and for that I am so thankful. If I think about people who I would never want to disappoint, you are on that list. How would you describe your journey and influence?*

ACB: "Thank you for that, that means so very much." It was not about me shining, it was about bringing out in my students what they could do well. As a teacher, you do not always know what your influence is, but when my second husband died due to COVID, I really realized what my impact may have been."

"When Mickey got extremely ill, he asked me to update people on Facebook about his progress, and I did that. When he died, I had to update Facebook. I had so many students who wrote to me on Facebook."

"One student wrote that I taught her how to love literature, and now you are teaching us how to grieve."

"I have realized in recent years that I am continuing to influence even though I am no longer teaching."

"My journey has taken me from a very young inexperienced teacher in a culture I did not know a lot about to a place where now I have real, human relationships with my students. You are not just my students; you were so much more than that. You all were invited to my wedding because we were together every day and I loved you all. The relationships went beyond "student-teacher," they transferred to "family.""

2.

DR. VIVIAN TOLBERT ROPER

Dr. *Roper is a legend in Kansas City, Missouri. She is an award-winning principal and school superintendent. I was blessed to work under her leadership while leading a K-8 school in Kansas City, MO.*

Dr. Roper is an award-winning school superintendent. She founded and for over twenty years led the Lee A. Tolbert Community Academy in Kansas City, Missouri as its first superintendent. I had the pleasant experience of working with her as her principal for four school years. She led with grace, tenacity, and perseverance. I learned so much from her during our time together.

LBC: *You have a highly successful tenure as a principal and school superintendent. To what do you attribute your success?*

VTR: "Thank you, Dr. C. I absolutely, without a doubt, first, attribute my success to the goodness of the Lord. I was determined to use Biblical principles throughout my work as an educator. My mantra is that school is about relationships, relationships, relationships... As a principal, I always tried to remember what it felt like to be a fifth-grade teacher - and made sure I listened and sought to understand the teacher's perspective as I dealt with policies and procedures. I always worked with the staff to establish norms that addressed the question: *What do you need from the group in order for you to perform at a stellar level?* And then, I modeled those norms consistently."

"The challenge is to be a light, not a judge; to be a model, not a critic." Stephen Covey.

"I spent hours building the team - overnight retreats, protocols that required team members to be part of the process in hiring others on the team — shared leadership was always the goal. Trust had to be built in order for commitment and loyalty to develop. In order to do that, we had to live by the norm: *If you have a problem with a person, go to the person! Come up with ideas to solve the problem and follow through; be truthful; let it stop with you; and timing (pick the right time to go to the person- definitely not when in anger).* Honesty, trust, and commitment were attributes I looked for and sought to develop in order to work with a solid team."

LBC: *Being a successful charter school superintendent is not an easy feat. What strategies helped you to navigate the charter school industry?*

VTR: "Prayer is an essential priority when working with people and institutions. Working with the charter school industry required much patience, perseverance, and networking. Politics play a part in charter school policies and laws. So, I go back to my "relationships" mantra. My brother, the founder of our charter school, had a relationship with the governor and other influential politicians in our state. He constantly wrote letters to influential persons in the system. He also headed a large regional organization of ministers in the area. We spent hours working with the local portion of community organizations that supported public charter schools- trust me, there were a lot of opponents! Building relationships with state department officials and local parent and ministerial groups were huge in navigating success as a not-for-profit charter school operator."

"Shared leadership with parents as partners is part of the title of the school. We *built* procedures that always included parents in the conversation regarding policies, etc. Today, we are entering our 25th year as a successful public charter school. Before opening, we were the first school in the area that required our teachers to participate in home visits before the first day of school. That was unheard of! And, Dr. Carpenter, we appreciate your input and efforts in our continued success."

"Creating an environment of welcoming teachers, parents, and students was also key to continued success. We focused on a theme that included teaching entrepreneurial skills to students, beginning in kindergarten! Children with that entrepreneurial mindset at an early age have a head start toward fulfilling their potential."

LBC: *I am so proud of how you are able to enjoy retirement. What advice do you have for young educators on planning for retirement?*

VTR: "Wow! What I can share with you is what has worked for me. My father taught me at the age of 15 to always put God first in my earnings. So, I have always paid tithes on my income. And let me tell you, it is a biblical principle, and I am a witness that it works!!"

"Also, young educators should take advantage of retirement plans that are offered by their districts. It may seem not so important when you are in your twenties, but trust me, if you are blessed with long life, you will enjoy the benefits! I worked 20 years in one district, then 20 years in a second district — I participated in the 401 plans, and I am soooo blessed today. I just recently returned from a cruise to Haiti, St. Thomas, and the Bahamas, and preparing to go on a 2024 cruise to see the Atlantic and Pacific Oceans merge. So, invest in a Roth IRA (if those are still available), make sure you have life insurance for you and your spouse (this is critical because if you get it while you are young and in good health, it is affordable — you may have to give up a few Starbucks coffees per month…).''

PART TWO
BUILDING BLOCKS

3.

MY CAREER START AS A TEACHER

I interviewed with Mr. Horace Dunson in November 1998 as I was finishing up student teaching. The teacher shortage was so great that student teachers who had proven to be on the right track could begin to interview for positions once seventy-five percent of the student teaching experience had been completed. If offered a position, the student teacher could be released from the field experience and immediately take over a classroom. During this time, teachers wore suits every day. I remember buying a new suit for the interview and feeling nervous as I walked into Salem Middle School in Lithonia, Georgia (Dekalb County School System). My memory allows me to see the front office as it was back then, along with Mr. Dunson's office. As nervous as I was, Mr. Dunson made me feel "at home."

Mr. Dunson is a tall, African-American male with a wide physique. I remember always looking at him and believing that he was strong and smart, and I was always impressed with his ability to be calm in all situations. I have known him for almost thirty years, and I do not believe that I have ever heard him raise his voice. He is a man of few words, but when he speaks, he speaks with experience, knowledge, and wisdom. People have always listened to Mr. Dunson; and I have always been impressed with his ability to think quickly and smartly even in the most fragile situations.

At the end of the interview, Mr. Dunson looked at me and looked at my resume and laughed to himself. I remember sitting there wondering what was so funny. He looked up at me and said, "How am I supposed to get in touch with you?" My eyes got bigger than they already are and as brown as my skin is, I know I turned red with embarrassment. I was thinking, "How could I forget to put a phone number on my resume?" Being the calm and reasonable person that he is, he simply stated, "it is ok, what is your number?" I remember rambling off my phone number because I was beating myself up on the inside. I worried that I would not get the job because he may have thought that I was careless or did not pay enough attention to detail. Mr. Dunson called me the next day and offered me my first teaching position. I graciously accepted. I think I screamed and jumped really high when I hung up the phone.

I was thankful that Mr. Dunson extended "grace" to me before any of us really knew the magnitude of the word.

I try to offer "grace" as I go about my life because I know that if the "grace" is handled responsibly, how it may change a life. During that moment, Mr. Dunson offered me a position to teach and influence children in the greatest profession of all time. He provided me with an opportunity to break a generational curse by choosing a profession that would allow me to achieve millionaire status. This moment of opportunity for me could contribute to the education of students and the development of schoolteachers by giving them the necessary tools to be the absolute best version of themselves by way of conversation, exposure, and opportunities.

Mr. Dunson was so amazing as a principal that I felt obligated to work for him in two school buildings - Salem Middle School and Martin Luther King, Jr. High School (both in Lithonia, GA). Even to this day, my colleagues who worked with me during those amazing times brag to each other whenever we interact with Mr. Dunson. We send pictures and videos to each other whenever we can spend time with him, and we are always jealous when he is spending time with one of our friends instead of with us. Mr. Dunson is a "legend" to us. We love him.

4.

MY BACKGROUND

I come from a two-parent home. My dad graduated from Washington High School in Atlanta, GA (ATL) and went off to the Army. He served in the Vietnam War. My mom will tell you my dad left the "ATL," "one way" and came back from Vietnam "different." He was not the same person. During my childhood, he would share bits and pieces of his experiences in the Army and Vietnam, but not too much. For the rest of his life, he dealt with the trauma of serving in Vietnam. As a child, I remember the traveling Vietnam Memorial Wall, and I vividly remember one year, my mom telling us we were going to see it. With all the naivety that a young child could muster, I became so excited to see this wall. I had no context about the Vietnam War and the harm it had caused so many Americans, but specifically African Americans. We never left the house that day. My dad stayed in bed all day. I did not realize that he could not handle seeing the wall. He was wise enough to know that going to see the wall would be an emotional trigger for him. He dealt with the trauma by way of nightmares, dabbling in crack-cocaine in the eighties, and having a fetish for women.

My dad also had a positive way of working through trauma and that was by way of running five miles a day. The saving grace for my dad was General Motors. He worked at General Motors for thirty-four years. Whenever my dad felt like 'he needed to go check himself in,' he did just that. General Motors never penalized him for going to get help. Through his trauma, he was able to keep and maintain a career with the largest auto maker in the world. He was able to seek mental health services when he needed them, and he was able to retire "well." My dad transitioned from his earthly home in 2012 and was finally able to find "peace." Although we immediately missed him, we knew that he was finally at peace and in a much better place than the earth had served him.

My mom was a devoted wife to my dad and later to my stepfather. My mom grew up in Buckhead, one of the most affluent communities in ATL. She graduated from Northside High School. During my mom and her sisters' experiences at Northside High School there were very few African American students. My mom can still name her African American classmates because there were ten of them at that time. My mom recalls one of her teachers telling her that she would never know how to cook because cooking required science and math. Unbeknownst to that teacher, my mom started cooking when she was six years old. She already knew how to cook. Not only was she already an amazing baker, but she could also cook before the teacher knew her name. *If you are ever blessed to sit at my mom's kitchen table (which is one of my most favorite places in the world), you will quickly learn that she is an amazing cook.* Shortly after my mom graduated from high school, while her younger sisters were still at Northside, they learned that the teachers were changing one of my aunt's grades. They did not want my aunt to make all A's because of the color of her skin. At that time, there were a number of white teachers who worked hard to keep African Americans out of honors classes and off the honor roll.

My mom worked in and retired from the insurance industry. She is an amazing, loving, and caring mom and "granny." She loves my sister and me with her whole being, but she adores her grandchildren. I have watched her love and support my sister, her grandchildren, and me in unimaginable ways. There is no way that any of us could call my mom in a time of need when she would not stop what she was doing and cater to us. Even when we ask her not to, she does, because that is what she loves to do. I have fond memories of my mom writing down her income and her expenses. She has always been meticulous about what bills needed to be paid and when they needed to be paid. As an adult when I followed her plan, I did well. Anytime I have deviated from her strategy, I have made

My BACKGROUND

mistakes. My mom is an amazing human being. I owe my whole life to her and all that she has taught me. Most importantly, I owe my mom for holding me accountable when I needed to hear the truth and see the light. Many people have told me during my life that my mom lets me do whatever I want to do, that she spoiled me, and she lets me get away with stuff. This is not true. I am so grateful that my mom chastises me when she needs to, holds me accountable when I make mistakes, and tells me the truth even when I do not want to hear any of it. I am most thankful that these conversations occur with my mom being calm, never raising her voice, and they happen in private. My mom always told me that we don't need witnesses to our conversations, "this is me and you."

I have many fond memories of spending time with both sides of my family while growing up. Our weekends were spent enjoying family, learning how to play all sorts of card games, playing pool, playing old-fashioned games outside, going to church together, and eating dinner together as a family. The "Thanksgiving-style family dinner" occurred on most Sundays during my childhood. I am grateful for such memories. These moments helped to shape who I am today and why I value "family" so much. I was taught and shown that if the family unit is "healthy," you work hard to keep it together. During my childhood and teenage years, I witnessed firsthand emotional and physical abuse, and was taught early on that such behavior should not be tolerated or accepted. I was also taught to "have my own," so that if I ever found myself in a situation that was unhealthy that I would have a means to escape and take care of myself. This is wise insight that proved to be valuable when I needed it most.

5.

MY CALLING

The school is my "safe" and "happy" place. My love for children is immeasurable. After stepping over into administration in 2007, I learned that my love for adults matches my energy and love for children. I have learned that I love to care for and help people. My number one mission is to help everyone that I encounter to be "better" than they were before we connected. If I don't leave you "better," I have failed at what I have been destined to accomplish.

I have a deep love for bringing people together. My entire mission is to create safe spaces in schools for adults to come to work and so students to come to school where everyone feels safe, cared for, and loved. I also want schools to be places where staff and scholars can share meals together, take care of their physical and mental health, talk and converse, share their goals, teach, learn, grow, and help one another along the way.

My life's work is dedicated to creating equitable spaces where adults and children want to take advantage of leaving their homes, their cars, and their hotel rooms; and also, to walk into their schools to learn and grow together. I am committed to establishing environments where adults and children, including staff, teachers, students, or parents, feel comfortable sharing their needs for food and clothing. My goal is to assist them in obtaining the necessary items for the evening and beyond, ensuring they have what they require for the days ahead.

My goal is to eliminate the belief of "I have to" and turn it into "I get to…"

For anyone reading this, I hope that you gain skills that you did not have before picking up this tool; it is full of strategies that you may use to help bring people together for the betterment of culture and society. My wish is that once you read this book you will put a whole lot of positive and intentional energy into creating a leadership legacy that can influence generations of children to transform into grateful, humble, influential, and resourceful adults.

PART THREE
STRATEGIES

Always move in "truth." Identify your core values and remember them, always.

6.

STAY TRUE TO SELF

My assistant principal experience occurred at the toughest school in the Dekalb County School System. I was assigned to McNair Middle School during a time where the entire staff had to interview for their positions. The Georgia Department of Education was threatening to take over the school if the district could not get it right in three years and I reported the third week of June when we had zero teachers on staff. The only staff that were in place were the custodians, the ISS paraprofessional, the security guard, and the cafeteria staff; and the district allowed one assistant principal to stay on site for the purpose of having some historical knowledge in the building. We had a lot of work to do with eight weeks of lag time. We were expecting one thousand middle school students to walk in the doors and learn about an entire staff, build relationships with us, trust us, and follow our lead.

We had a veteran principal who was new to the school, a seasoned assistant principal who had decades of experience in the community, a new male assistant principal, and me. We had no choice but to immediately like and respect each other because we were charged to get it right, or else. Although I grew up two highway exits from this community, this was new territory for me. Whereas in the community I grew up in my classmates and I aspired to be engineers, teachers, lawyers, actors, actresses, entrepreneurs, etc., this community of students wanted to be rappers, strippers, drug dealers, or go to a league… any league. The league that they aspired to go to did not matter if it was connected to a ball, or a song, as long as it was connected to a millionaire-type check. I was so shocked at the behavior of the parents. It was during this experience that I was called a "bit**" for the first time in my life. My reaction was to only look at the mom and say, "ok."

Working in that type of environment was stressful and intense. I often remember going home feeling so exhausted that all I could do was sleep and wake up the next day and do it all over again. I remember hearing people say, "it does not take all of that." It took all of that and then some; however, I grew to love the community, the students, the parents, and the staff. I was not able to save them all, but I did help a few to stay on the right track and make good lives for themselves.

Due to the status of the student achievement levels, a "state facilitator" was assigned to the school and I had the honor of working with Dr. Aretha Pigford. Dr. Pigford and I became very close friends and spent a lot of time together outside of school. She had served as a superintendent in South Carolina, and I clearly remember her telling me one day, "do not let the environment change you, stay true to yourself." I immediately knew why she told me that, because working in tough environments can sometimes make you tough. I consider myself "strong." I don't consider myself "tough." There is a difference between "strong" and "tough." I simply said, "yes ma'am."

I remember reflecting on that conversation many times over the course of my career. On many occasions, I have reminded myself to not allow people, situations, environments, or circumstances to change who I am. My mental and physical make-up is what it is, and I love it. Oftentimes, I have reminded myself of this conversation, and in some of the most difficult circumstances, it has allowed me to stay "grounded" and "centered" in my truth.

In all schools, in all situations, and with all people, I encourage you to "stay true to self."

*I've always believed that our greatest
rewards come from serving others.*

7.

DON'T WORRY ABOUT THE DATA, WORRY ABOUT THE PEOPLE

During the last twenty-five years of this journey, I have yet to wake up and think about a test, other than the logistics of administering the assessment. I have woken up in the middle of the night and I have woken up on many mornings worried about and thinking about students, teachers, and the staff who make up the school. As a school leader, I am privy to personal information about people. Sometimes, this information is extremely sensitive. People share with me because if they feel like they are not performing their best and have a reason, they want me to know. Parents come in and share about life-changing situations that may affect their child, and they want me to know, so that support can be provided to their child. There are many reasons why information is shared. Oftentimes, the conversations end, but my worrying does not. I care about people. Despite various backgrounds and personalities, I have grown to love my staff and my students. I grow to immensely care about their livelihood, their performance in and out of the classroom, the way they show up on the field and the court, and I want them to know just how deep my concern is because it is important to me that they know they are unique individuals to me.

As a school leader, it is important to learn what and who my staff cares about and to understand just how deep the love truly is, thus as I get to know the children and pets of my staff and hear about their stories and experiences, I also begin to love and care for their children and their pets. When a child gets hurt, or becomes sick, and my staff member is worried, I worry. When their child performs well in the classroom, has a great project, or has a good game, I am also cheering them on. If their pet gets sick, or must have surgery, or they have to put their pet "down," I share their pain. This connection is important.

I never want anyone to spend their days stressing or worrying, but if we must worry; let's worry about the people and not the assessment.

You are encouraged to not worry about the data but to think carefully and love your people.

*Love is feeling safe,
no matter where you are.*

8.

MAKE SCHOOL A "SAFE" SPACE FOR EVERYONE

The scientific experts have traced the start of COVID to Wuhan, China in 2019, and the conversation about this horrible disease and outbreak began in The United States in January 2020. Like many Americans, I did not pay much attention to the initial news stories of the outbreak. I was living in Kansas City, Missouri at the time and was employed as the principal of the Lee A. Tolbert Community Academy. During the weeks of late February leading into March 2020, several staff members began to wear masks and a few parents had begun to send their students to school in masks. Although I knew this was a deadly virus, I did not believe that it would shut the world down and make everyone across the world stop what they were doing as it relates to work and school and thus become confined to their home. I had no clue this was going to happen. As the initial discussions began about shutting down schools, I remember having conversations with my staff about preparing to have an extended Spring Break, but we were all sure that after two or three weeks, school and life would resume as normal. It did not take but a few days of Spring Break to realize that we were not going back to school any time soon.

Once the reality had set in, that school was closed for an indefinite amount of time, I tried my best to ensure that my children felt as safe as possible in this very unpredictable and unforeseen time. None of us had ever seen or experienced being so limited in what we could do, where we could go, and who we could be around. At this point I had not lived near my family in seven years, but I always knew that I could get to them if I needed or wanted to, I knew I had the flexibility of catching a flight or gassing up a car whenever I chose to, but the mere thought of not being able to move was quite frightening. I believe what added to the level of fright was the mere fact that no one knew how long the isolation would last.

Additionally, while we were home, confined to the television, we were exposed to the killing of George Floyd. The United States of America has a history of mistreating African Americans. However, mis-treatment was often told to us by way of family; and if we were fortunate to grow up in a community like I did, it was told to us by our teachers. The teachers at Southwest Dekalb High School did not hold back.

They told us the truth. They wanted us to know what we were walking into as high school graduates. During my high school experience, there were times when our teachers "talked." Yes, they actually talked to us about life. There were times when we didn't open a textbook or pull out a piece of paper. If our teachers felt like a "lesson" needed to be taught, you sat down, they talked, and you listened. If one of us did something during a class change that they did not like, the whole class got a lecture. The "lesson" transferred to a "life" lesson.

Again, it was "told" to us. Although by 2020, most people were aware and conscious of the fact that our country still had a lot of work to do because we were still mourning Travyon Martin, Daunte Wright, Freddie Gray, Cameron Lamb, Tamir Rice, Philando Castile, Breonna Taylor, Ahmaud Arbery, and countless others. These were stories that were told and shared after they had happened. Additionally, although we were mourning the lives of these young African American souls, our lives were still in motion. We were still going to work, waiting in car lines, picking up kids, visiting our family, etc. Our lives were still going on; so, although we were mourning these tragic deaths, our conversations were limited to when we had breaks to discuss and debate. But that was not the case with George Floyd. Due to Covid, everyone's life was paused, and we *had* to pay attention to the killing of George Floyd.

George Floyd

Although the video was released after it happened, it allowed us to witness exactly *how* it happened. The video cannot lie and did not lie. The video told the truth. For over nine minutes, a white police officer kneeled on the neck of George Floyd, an African American and caused him to die.

Because of COVID, we were home, confined to our TVs. We could not hide from George Floyd. The only choice was to experience this horrible and tragic death, that, was completely avoidable. We experienced the death of George Floyd every single time the television was on.

During that time, I was so thankful that I lived in a safe neighborhood where I could sit on a porch or go for a long walk. I was extremely grateful that I could take my kids on long walks and spend time outside. Additionally, I fell in love with my exercise equipment all over again. Although this was such an unpredictable time, I was so grateful to have what I needed and I learned that I wanted to continue to create a space where I had everything that I needed, what I loved, and some of what I enjoyed right at home. I started making mental lists of what I did not have, but what I would work to have right at home. Since COVID "happened to us," I have told myself that if anything like this happens again, I will be very prepared because I am constantly working to try to have everything I need, all of what I love, and some of what I want "right at home." Some of the things that make me feel safe are family, friends, comfortable housing, food, exercise equipment, warm and cozy blankets, positive messages all around, pictures of family and friends, and a remote control. All of what I just stated makes me feel "safe."

At some point, I asked myself why don't we do this in schools? Since COVID, I have tried to ensure that schools are safer than they have ever been. If I am going to work hard to make sure the home is safe, I should do the same thing for the school that I am responsible for and I am making it my business to do just that for all the students that are under my care. If their parents are going to trust me to care for them, I am going to take the responsibility seriously. I want each child to enter and exit and always feel safe and have what they need, what they love, and some of what they like. This begins with learning about the students and understanding their interests. If they want a kickball team, let me find someone to lead it and if they want flag football, let me figure that out as well. If you are my student and you tell me you want to act, let me find someone who can teach you the skills of acting. If one of my female students walks up to me and tells me she needs a menstrual pad, I take her to my office, and I give her one. I do not send her to the nurse, I go ahead and take care of it. Why do I need to send her to the nurse and all she is requesting is a menstrual pad? My thought process is come here, "I got you, now go back to class, and be GREAT."

I also know that I serve students who did not have the luxury of a warm bed and food on the table, thus, keeping a clothing closet and a food pantry is an absolute must. From my vantage point, we can't have school if we don't have a food pantry and a clothing closet.

Once the student expresses to me what they need, it is my responsibility to give it to them each day and to make them feel "safe" in their learning environment.

You are encouraged to make school a "safe" space for everyone, every single day.

It's good to be Blessed.
It's better to be a Blessing.

9.

BE A "BLESSING" TO EVERYONE ON THIS JOURNEY

Having the opportunity to lead a school is a "blessing." I do not take it for granted. I am super grateful to every single district office administrator that has trusted me and continues to trust me to lead a school.

I first became a principal in 2007.

During the winter break of 2006, I called my principal and told her that I wanted to begin pursuing the principalship, that I would begin to submit applications, and that I wanted her support.

Her response was, "Why do you want to leave me so bad?"

All I could think at the time was, *how is this middle-aged woman upset that I want to pursue a goal that I have set for myself?* At that moment, I promised myself to never be that person. At that very moment, I promised myself that if anyone ever picked up the phone to share their dream or goal with me, I would do everything in my power to help him or her.

At that very moment, I thought how selfish it is to think of one's own personal desires when another person takes the time to pick up the phone and share their dreams with you.

My response was, "it has nothing to do with you. I believe that I am ready, and I want to pursue the opportunity."

Three years later, she called me to apologize. I accepted her apology.

This experience taught me what not to do.

I submitted applications for principal vacancies in South Carolina and Georgia. I was so comfortable in my hometown of "Atlanta" and "Decatur," and I could have pursued the principalship right at home. But I wanted to go somewhere where no one knew my name and establish myself as a leader.

One school district that I interviewed with sent a team to where I was currently serving. I was working at McNair Middle School (Dekalb County School System) at the time. This generation calls it "popping up." The team "popped up on me." I remember my security guard calling me on my cell phone and his exact words were, "DOC, come here, these folk are asking about you." I did not know what he was talking about. I proceeded to walk to the front office.

They wanted to speak to teachers that worked with me.

The principal selected teachers for the team to interview. They spoke to teachers on the staff and asked about my character, my decision-making, and my ability as a school leader.

In the spring of 2007, I was offered positions in several districts in South Carolina and Georgia. I chose Bibb County in Macon, GA.

Working in the Bibb County School System was an awesome experience. I met some of the most amazing students and teachers. There were several of us who began the 2007-2008 school year as first-year principals, and we remain friends today. We were first-year principals leading schools during a recession. Thus, we were leading schools during extremely tough financial and political times.

During my time in Bibb County, I learned so much. "School Improvement" was a "thing" and if you were not improving a school, there was a problem. I was assigned to King-Danforth Elementary School and the demographics were very similar to McNair Middle School. During my first year at King-Danforth we were designated as an "America's Choice" School and I distinctly remember the Deputy Superintendent, Sylvia McGee calling me and telling me that she believed I could "turn this school around."

I had no clue what she meant, but I agreed with her.

This woman had just drove to Decatur a few months ago, picked my teachers apart about me, and offered me a position. How could I disappoint this beautiful soul?

I was thinking, *"OK." You got "it."*

I went to work, and my teachers went to work. One task was to go to training. There were several trainings on-site, but there were also several trainings "off-site."

I remember telling the staff that we were going to Los Angeles, California for the America's Choice conference and announcing who I was going to take to represent our school. Everyone cheered for the opportunity.

Two of my staff members that were chosen were integral in our transition to an America's Choice school and they were performing at a remarkably high level. I was so proud of them for their growth.

After our staff meeting where I announced who was going to L.A., one of my most integral staff members came up to me and whispered in my ear, "I am scared to fly. I cannot do this."

I was dumbfounded because from where I come from, where I was raised, we do not know to sit down, we like to "go." We like to "fly." I simply said, "NO problem." "I got you."

She said, "Ok." We locked eyes, and I knew she was scared.

I knew I had to teach her how to "fly."

That flight from Atlanta to Los Angeles is still vivid in my mind today. I booked my teachers' flights so they could sit in the same row. As we pulled off the tarmac in Atlanta, they were holding hands. I looked over at one teacher who was so afraid, she closed her eyes and held the hands of her friends. She trusted her friends.

She trusted me.

A few years later, she sent me a text expressing gratitude. "Thank you." She said, "I have learned to love to travel, and I cannot stay off of a plane." She said, "I love you for teaching me how to do this." I remember this text conversation almost twenty years later.

This experience taught me that school leadership is not just about teaching kids and helping kids to perform high on an annual state assessment, but it is also about pouring into the adults that take care of the kids.

When I think about the greatness of this leadership journey, all I can do is to be "thankful" that I was given the opportunity to not only be a "blessing" to some, but to also experience my own blessings from others.

Use your role as a way to bless others.

Walking in gratitude will make one understand that a bad moment is just that, and it should not transform into a bad day, or a bad week. Having a feeling of gratitude from the moment we wake up until we end our day will help ordinary moments feel like magnificent milestones.

10.

WALK IN WITH GRATITUDE

The mere fact that when I walk into a school, I can influence and change lives is my ultimate "high."

Do you mean, I get to "change a life today?" I get the opportunity to motivate a teacher or pump up a coach! I get to greet a scholar in the most magnificent way possible to make them feel welcome and loved at my school?! I absolutely love the opportunity that I get to do this on a daily basis.

Each school day morning, I am so excited to do this all over again.

"Let's GO" is my daily mantra.

I LOVE WHAT I DO AND I LOVE THAT I GET TO WALK IN MY SCHOOL BUILDING WITH SO MUCH GRATITUDE. There is absolutely nothing to be upset about. My teachers are working. My scholars are eager, and I am here. I am right where I am supposed to be.

Leading a school is not a chore for me. This is my life's work. This is my calling. I absolutely love my teachers. I absolutely love my staff. I absolutely love my scholars. There is no other place I would rather be.

I am so thankful for my current district leadership. I am surrounded by visionary leaders who have a purpose and understand how to stay focused on the goals and the vision of the organization.

When you walk in with gratitude, you walk in happy, and the energy extends to the scholars.

Oftentimes, I encounter students that are rolling their eyes, have their lips poked out, or are rolling their necks, and I say, "why?" I smile as I am talking to them and asking them what is wrong, and I offer a hug, they lean in, and all is well with the world. They will sometimes laugh because they know they had nothing to be upset about in the first place. Or they realize that they do have a valid reason to be upset, but I help them to figure out how to "shake it off," so that they can focus on school.

When you walk in with gratitude, a feeling of happiness and abundance takes over, and it extends to the scholars.

Family should be the place where you can be your most complete self.

Where you're accepted and appreciated, seen, and valued, even in moments of disagreement.

It should be your soft place to fall, the place where you're reminded that no matter what happens to you, in the face of your deepest challenges, you are loved.
   - **Oprah Winfrey**

11.

CREATE A FAMILY

Since the start of my career, I have worked in many school systems. In Georgia, I have worked in the following school districts: Dekalb, Bibb, Newton, and currently Richmond. In Missouri, I gained experience in private and charter schools. Regardless of where I was, it has always been and continues to be my goal to create a family.

Very recently, I was at a basketball game on a Saturday and my children wanted something to eat from the concession stand and I did not have any cash on me. One of my coaches overhead the conversation and gave my daughter a twenty-dollar bill. I said, "are you sure?" She said, "we are family."

I smiled and said, "thank you."

A few weeks later, one of my teachers sent me a text asking me if I had cash because he wanted to go to the concession stand. Again, we were at a basketball game. I was so happy to tell him, "yes."

I could return the favor!

Supporting our teachers and students by way of showing up in their classrooms to support them as well as attending sporting and club events is extremely important and sends the message that we care about them as a scholar, but also as an athlete and participant. Love is a verb, and it is demonstrated by our actions. It is important that we treat our teachers and students like family.

When the school operates in a family-like atmosphere, everyone genuinely cares for each other. We may not always get along, we may not always agree, but we care and love each other, and we do not mean any harm to one another. This is family.

Sometimes we are glad to see one another and sometimes we are glad when the day is over, so we can get a break from each other. However, we look forward to seeing each other again the next day. This is family. Schools that operate like a family generally have fewer discipline problems, stronger relationships, and a positive climate and culture.

"Family is everything." …. "Even in the school."

Leaders should be courageous and understand when to hit the courageous button.

12.

BE COURAGEOUS

Sometimes we have the wrong people in our classrooms teaching our children. Parents send the best that they have to us every day and they expect us to teach, lead, inspire, coach, and mentor their child(ren). Our scholars should go home feeling even more loved and cared for than they did when they entered the school building. As a school leader, when I witness teachers loving, caring, and disciplining children, it warms my heart because I know they are truly invested in the growth of the child. Children and teens thrive and grow when they spend their entire school day surrounded by loving and caring adults.

There are times when we identify people who are in the wrong field. During my leadership journey, I have had the experience of working with and coming into contact with adults who have simply made the wrong career choice. These adults may have had good intent, but they are not passionate about teaching children and/or they have very unrealistic expectations for children. Such identifications and interactions call for courageous conversations.

During the recession years, somewhere around 2009 or 2010, I remember interviewing a highly intelligent male teacher candidate. He was a real estate agent, and due to the recession, he needed a job with more stability than what the real estate market could provide at the time. During his interview, he clearly expressed the fact that he really did not like children, but due to the market he needed a job that would be "easy."

There is absolutely nothing about teaching children that is "easy."

The best thing we can do for our children is to remove adults from their lives who are not passionate about the mission of helping and improving the lives of those children. We must be very honest with adults who have made the wrong career move.

During these courageous moments of leadership, we have to encourage, and sometimes help people find their way to the other side of the school.

Thinking with clarity through the decision-making process is the best strategy for solid and strategic movement for academic excellence.

13.

TAKE TIME TO "PAUSE" AND "THINK"

There will be times when school administration has to make immediate decisions. Various levels of emergencies will arise and impact on school operations. Oftentimes, teachers and administrators are faced with questions and scenarios that call for impromptu decision-making. However, oftentimes, questions arise, situations abound, and ideas are presented that do not call for such intense leadership.

Thus, staff and parents will often expect an immediate response upon asking a question or presenting an idea. However, if it is a situation that can cause a ripple effect of other aspects of the school, it is wise to take a "pause" and "think" through each situation and scenario. When I am training a new school administrator, I take time to teach them the "pause and think" strategy aka "PT." Oftentimes, teachers and students will ask administrators questions with great ideas and great activities, but there may very well be the possibility of a negative ripple effect. Sometimes, the ideas can be as serious as an idea that can impact the master schedule or something as simple as a change to "field" day. Either way, if the idea is not presented with clarity, and the idea is not thought through systematically, there can be room for a huge mistake or a negative outcome that can impact the entire school.

I often tell my staff to take a moment for some "PT." I encourage my staff to be brave and tell people, "Let me take a moment to think through this." Every question does not have to have an immediate response. Take a moment to "pause," "think," and "reflect."

Answer questions with a clear mental space. Clarity helps us think "strong" and "wise." We cannot lead schools with a "strong and wrong" mentality.

"Strong" and "wise" win every time.

Lead from the inside.

14.

MAKE IT "HEARTWORK"

During a business meeting of a service organization that I belong to, one of the leaders in the organization was running for office; and during her campaign speech, she explained that serving the organization is "HEARTWORK" for her. This term has resonated with me since I heard it for the first time a few years ago. It is my truest belief that the work of education is my passion. Serving schools as a principal is my "calling." Through the role of the principalship I can help adults and children every single day and there is nothing else that I would rather do.

If you are currently in the field of education and you have found this to be "your place," and this is your "heartwork" continue to make it meaningful for children. Just as if you are in the field of education and you have realized this is not the industry for you, do yourself and your students a favor and make a different career move. Those people that stay in education with no meaningful purpose and little to no passion for children and teens hurt generations of children emotionally and psychologically. Unfortunately, the level of hurt that a child experiences from an uncaring teacher will transfer to elevated levels of trauma that will manifest itself through unhealthy behaviors. Additionally, we should work hard to create experiences and moments in school that will make students grateful for their teachers and school leaders. As school leaders, we should strive to create opportunities for students so that when they look back as adults they smile and receive the memories with thankfulness and happiness.

It has always been my priority to not be the teacher or leader that students can share negative experiences about, and I never want to hurt a child emotionally. Words in our schools matter. Conversations in our schools matter. Behaviors in our schools matter.

I always try to move about the school with "heartwork."

Those of us who have found our calling in this amazing field have proven to help generations of children and those children turn into amazing adults, and they come back and tell us how we helped them through something that we had no clue we were helping them through.

When we are centered in our work with meaningful intent and purpose and attempt every decision with a "heartwork" mindset, we will forever be able to reach, teach, and inspire children and adults for years to come.

To be effective, leaders have to work through their trauma.

15.

GET HELP

It is not enough to encourage others to work on themselves and not take time to work on "self."

The best thing that we can do for the staff and scholars that we lead is to get help, however we need it. We can give our schools the best form of leadership when we are our best self. As school leaders, we should make it our business to get in the best emotional, spiritual, and physical health that we possibly can. As I am completing the experience of writing this book, I realize that I have "new" trauma that has been stacked on top of "old" trauma and I must make it my priority to get the help that I need so that I do not go about my day hurting others. The worst thing that any of us can do is to ignore our ills and act as though they do not exist.

Historically, in the African American community, therapy has been resisted and even frowned upon. The practice of not telling anyone your business is pervasive in the Black community. In recent years, the stigma has begun to be lifted as an increasing number of African Americans have become more educated on the benefits of mental health support and the practice of therapy.

Very recently, I had a bad dream, but the dream involved behavior that happened to me in real life. In this dream I was ridiculed, called names, and picked on over and over until I woke up in a panic. I woke up sweating and had a headache because of the dream. It was at this moment that I knew it was time to reach out for help. I know I cannot be the best version of myself for my kids or my school if I do not get the assistance that I desperately need.

Taking advantage of the mental health experts and resources that are available to us is imperative to creating healthy and inspiring spaces everywhere we go. It is necessary to pause and get support and help so that we can continue to grow personally and mature into the best educators that we can possibly become. This is a perfect step to creating safe spaces for our scholars and our educators.

LAQUANDA CARPENTER

SPEAKER | CHANGE AGENT | THOUGHT LEADER

LaQuanda Carpenter, an esteemed educational pioneer with two decades of experience, is dedicated to shaping academic success and advancing equity through teacher empowerment. Her unwavering dedication to dynamic school cultures has established her as a leading authority in her field. She ignites transformative change by inspiring educators, nurturing inclusive learning environments, and pioneering innovative curriculum strategies. LaQuanda strives to share her expertise at conferences that unite educational leaders. Her passion extends to collaborating with organizations devoted to women's empowerment and forging meaningful connections with non-profits and educational entities.

SPEAKING TOPICS

- Leading with Purpose: Equity in Education
- Navigating the Future of Education
- Empowering Leaders to Bridge the Gap
- Shaping School Cultures: A Blueprint for Success
- Vision-Driven Leadership for Educational Excellence
- Championing Change & Unlocking HER Power

AFFILIATIONS

GLISI • Missouri EDUCATION • ascd

TRAINING DESCRIPTION

These dynamic sessions provide an opportunity to learn about teacher empowerment and innovative strategies that are transforming the future of education. Gain insights, tools, and inspiration to drive positive change in classrooms and beyond. Book LaQuanda today!

BOOKING INFORMATION

Email: Carpela1@boe.richmond.k12.ga.us

Call: 706-799-6656

www.linkedin.com/in/laquanda-carpenter/